THE CRASH OF '29
AND THE NEW DEAL

Turning Points in American History

THE CRASH OF '29 AND THE NEW DEAL

Bruce Glassman

Silver Burdett Company, Morristown, New Jersey

Cincinnati; Glenview, Ill.; San Carlos, Calif.;
Dallas; Atlanta; Agincourt, Ontario

Reginald Marsh

Acknowledgements

We would like to thank the following people for reviewing the manuscript and for their guidance and helpful suggestions: Professor Kenneth Kusmer, Department of History, Temple University; and Diane Sielski, Library Media Coordinator, Coldwater Village Exempted Schools, Coldwater, Ohio.

Cover, Title-page and Contents page photos courtesy of the Library of Congress.

Library of Congress Cataloging-in-Publication Data

Glassman, Bruce.
 The crash of '29 and the New Deal.

 (Turning points in American history)
 Bibliography: p.
 Includes index.
 Summary: Examines the period of American history beginning with the Roaring Twenties and the disastrous stock market crash of 1929 and ending with financial rebuilding through the New Deal and World War II.
 1. United States — History — 1919–1933 — Juvenile literature.   2. Depressions — 1929 — United States — Juvenile literature.   3. New Deal, 1933–1939 — Juvenile literature.   4. United States — History — 1933–1945 — Juvenile literature.
 [1. Depressions — 1929.   2. United States — History — 1919–1933.   3. United States — History — 1933–1945]
 I. Title.   II. Series.
 E784.G52   1986   973.91   85-40172
 ISBN 0-382-06831-9
 ISBN 0-382-06978-1 (softcover)

 Created by Media Projects Incorporated

Series design by Bruce Glassman
Bernard Schleifer, Design Consultant
Ellen Coffey, Project Editor
Jeffrey Woldt, Photo Research Editor
Charlotte A. Freeman, Photo Research Associate

Published simultaneously in Canada by GLC/Silver Burdett Publishers

Manufactured in the United States of America

CONTENTS

INTRODUCTION

PANIC

Wall Street is located near the southern tip of Manhattan Island, in New York City. It is the site of the New York Stock Exchange and the financial center of the United States. The Wall Street area is in the oldest settled district in New York, and its narrow streets and stately architecture give it the look of an old European capital, in contrast to the patchwork of commercial and residential neighborhoods to the north.

In the late morning of Thursday, October 24, 1929, noisy crowds began to fill the narrow lanes outside the Stock Exchange. At first glance, this might have

October 17, 1929. Across from the New York Stock Exchange, investors anxiously wait for news as the market crashes.

been another of those mass celebrations—say, at news of the Armistice eleven years before, or at the return of aviator Charles A. Lindbergh just two years earlier. But these crowds had not gathered for celebration; they had gathered for news of what was going on inside the Exchange, to hear confirmations or denials of the news that stocks "across the board" were rapidly losing their value.

At about 11 A.M., people in the crowd noticed a man atop one of the buildings near the Exchange. Soon more and more people looked up and noticed, and pointed. The police were summoned. The man atop the building, it turned out, was a building-maintenance worker going about his job, but the crowd had assumed he was

a stockbroker or financier preparing to jump—to follow the path of his fortunes.

Even in 1929, news—especially financial news—traveled fast. Fluctuations in stock prices were computed as stocks were bought and sold on the "floor" of the New York Stock Exchange, and these prices were reported almost instantly on ticker-tape machines as the day wore on. On this October Thursday, in brokerage offices throughout the country, the news coming over the tickers was alarming, and by noon, confused reports were appearing in late-edition newspapers and on the radio.

At the heart of the panic of October 24, 1929, were rapidly falling stock prices and investors' fears that prices would not soon recover. A look at the day-to-day workings of the stock market will help to set the scene for this unprecedented loss of confidence in American business.

A business requires money to establish facilities, to buy machinery, to advertise and promote its products and to expand and improve existing plants and operations. Instead of borrowing from a bank the large sums of money needed to support

Façade of the New York Stock Exchange as it looks today.

these ventures, the company sells, to anyone who wishes to buy, a "share" of stock in the business. The share is, in effect, an "IOU" given to the investor for the amount invested. As it would to a bank, the company pays interest to the investor on the invested money. The interest payments, usually sent every three or six months, are called "dividends." Unlike interest payments to a bank, which are often fixed, dividends basically rise and fall according to the rise and fall of the company's profits. This way, the investor is sharing in the success or failure of the company.

Many people invest their money in stocks rather than depositing it in a bank. The bank pays a safe, fixed, guaranteed rate of interest, whereas a company, if it performs well, usually rewards its shareholders with dividends that are higher than the rate of interest offered by a bank. If the corporation does poorly, however, the dividends can be much lower than the interest rate offered by a bank—or the corporation can choose to pay no dividends at all. Thus, in a sense, investment in the stock market is a gamble.

Since the dividends paid by a company increase when the company is reaping greater profits, the value, and consequently the selling price, of that stock increases as well. When a stock becomes more valuable, more people wish to buy it. It appears, after all, to be a good investment. In keeping with the new demand for a stock, the selling price rises.

There are basically two types of buyers in the stock market: investors and speculators. Investors usually buy shares in companies that show stability over time. It is their hope that dividends will rise with the increased success of their "partner."

Speculators, on the other hand, are less concerned with the long-term success of a particular company. Instead they hope for sudden increases in the value of a stock after they have purchased it. The strategy of speculation is usually to buy stock in a company early in its history, before demand for the stock drives up its price. Thus the speculator "buys low," expecting other buyers to follow in large enough numbers to drive up the stock's price. At some point, when the speculator suspects the stock's price to have gone as high as it is

The floor of the New York Stock Exchange, c. 1920.

likely to go, he or she "sells high," and makes a profit.

The practice of widespread speculation, as we will see, can be dangerous. And the great increase in stock-market speculation during the late 1920s, particularly in 1929, was a major factor in the rapid collapse of the market on this soon-infamous Thursday in October.

Back at the New York Stock Exchange on October 24, 1929, the usually hectic scene on the floor, with brokers and traders calling out purchase and selling orders, was now described by one onlooker as a "wild scramble." As prices of stocks continued to fall, brokers were receiving orders to sell faster than they could possibly process them. Several brokers were seen moving about the floor with wastebaskets full of sell-order slips. By early afternoon, the tickertape itself was unable to keep pace with the rate of stock sales and the accompanying rate of falling prices. Brokers were now selling their clients' investments without knowing the current price or value of those investments. Still the orders to sell poured in, and the panic fed upon itself and intensified.

By afternoon of this "Black Thursday," the scene of the gathering throng on Wall Street was being replayed in scaled-down versions across the nation, in the downtowns of other cities and outside storefront brokerage offices on the Main Streets of smaller towns. These scenes were wholly foreign to the crowds who took part in them. The sight of so many people gathered for purposes other than celebration was alarming. One reporter on the scene in New York described it as "the worst catastrophe to be visited on the continent since the Civil War."

Rumors circulated. It was said that there had been eleven suicides in a matter of hours in New York City. The Chicago and New York Exchanges were said to have been closed indefinitely. Federal troops had been called into lower Manhattan to restore order. . . . None of these reports was true, but all of them told of the panic that was spreading as investors large and small scurried to sell their stake in American business, to get out before the last dollar was gone.

1

EVERY MAN A MILLIONAIRE

Still reeling from the savage effects of World War I, Americans by the early 1920s were ready to return to a happy and peaceful existence. The "return to normalcy," which Warren G. Harding promised as Republican presidential nominee in 1920, was just what the country craved. A new belief in the values of isolationism became the popular approach, and Americans yearned ever more for the simple pleasures offered to them in their great land.

Aiding Americans in their quest for contentment was the great postwar "pros-

Warren G. Harding

perity boom." Soon dubbed the "Roaring Twenties," the decade provided Americans with new opportunities. The now booming automobile industry not only provided thousands with a new mobility but offered employment as well. The greater demand for automobiles created demands for increased production of rubber, copper, glass, steel, road paving, and oil and gas. Although fewer than 7 million passenger cars were registered in the U.S. in 1919, the figures would soon grow by more than 1 million per year, providing more than 4 million people with jobs. Other industries enjoyed prosperity as well. Those producing rayon, cigarettes, household applian-

ces, telephones, and cosmetics all thrived during this period.

The increasing growth in motion-picture technology sparked continued progress in the entertainment industry, and Americans quickly fell in love with this new form of diversion. Radio, by 1922, had become a craze. Sales that year of radios and related accessories totaled $60 million (a great sum in those days). With industry booming and most of America employed, a feeling of great optimism swept the country. The "American dream" seemed to be working.

But what was making the United States so prosperous? After the war, which had ravaged Europe and left North America untouched, U.S. factories and industries were still geared up for the high rate of production necessitated by the war. Now that the war was over, the factories found the transition from wartime production of tanks, planes, and guns to peacetime production of automobiles and other goods an easy one.

Our young country, with its enormous natural and human resources, found itself ready to gear its production toward the improvement of life at home. The new abundance of jobs gave more Americans money to spend. And the money they spent helped to keep America's industries growing.

Along with this new prosperity and increased buying power came a newly popular phenomenon that even further enhanced the ability of Americans to consume. This was "installment" buying, or credit buying. Created primarily to give people greater incentives to buy, credit purchasing added an entirely new dimension to the American marketplace. No longer were consumers limited to buying items solely with the money in their pockets. Soon, four out of every five cars in the U.S. would be bought on installment plans. Homes and other goods would soon be purchased in the same way.

The advantages of credit soon made themselves obvious to those who worked on the Stock Exchange. Seeing the growing participation of Americans in the stock market, brokers created what was called "buying on margin." If one wanted to purchase stock, one could call a stockbroker (an individual who buys and sells stocks on the Exchange on behalf of the investors and speculators) and ask his advice about finding an affordable stock to purchase. Once a prospective buyer was ready to invest, the broker encouraged the

"Flappers," dancing in the style which outraged the older generation.

investment by offering to extend a line of credit, called "margin." The buyer would then be able to purchase a number of stocks without having to put down the full value of the shares.

For example, Mr. Smith wishes to buy one hundred dollars' worth of a certain stock. If he buys on margin, he will have to give his broker only $40. The broker will then supply the remaining $60 and buy the $100 in stock in Mr. Smith's name. Mr. Smith then waits for his stock to rise, perhaps to twice its value from the time of his purchase. Mr. Smith can now tell his broker to sell the stock for $200, regain his original $40 investment, pay his broker the $60 extended on margin, and still retain $100 in pure profit. The actions of both the investor and the broker rely heavily on the confidence that the stock will, in fact, rise. The system, during a time of prosperity, might seem easy and foolproof. Thus, during the 1920s, speculation boomed, and anyone who did not "play the market" was considered quite foolish.

With prosperity throughout the nation and a firm belief that things would only get better, the U.S. saw a change in its moral practices as well—a rebellion against the strict codes of behavior prevalent in pre-war America. Many of these changes were a direct result of the worldly experiences of American soldiers returning home from the battlefields and cities of Europe. In the U.S., women's fashions now called for hemlines about nine inches off the ground. In 1921, a group of legislators in Utah attempted to pass a law that would have provided for a fine and imprisonment of women wearing skirts in public "higher than three inches over the ankle." No longer did young men and women dance far apart. Now the popular dances had them cheek to cheek in what, to many, was an obvious display of moral decay. Dance bands replaced the romantic and soothing music of the violin with the wailing and explosive sound of the saxophone.

This time of moral change was also characterized by the growing independence of women, who had won suffrage (the right to vote) in 1920, and, in part, by the new flow of European ideas about psychology and sex that were now being heard in America. A new voice, that of Sigmund Freud, was being heard by many for the first time. Freud's theories about sex and its relation to all human behavior helped to destroy many of the taboos surrounding the mere discussion of the subject.

Dr. Anna Shaw and Ms. Carrie Chapman Catt lead 20,000 suffragettes down New York City's Fifth Avenue, 1918.

Though some Americans were convinced that everyone was enjoying boundless success, there were many who did not share in this great age of affluence. The American farmer was one who did not have a place at the great banquet of prosperity.

During World War I, American farmers supplied food not only to the United States, but to most of a war-torn Europe on the edge of starvation. The demand for food was so great that the American farmer, on the average, had increased his yearly output by 15 percent per year. For a short time after the war, demand continued to remain high. But when European farmers began to resume production, the demand for American farm products dropped sharply. With the great drop in demand came a great excess of supply. And with the excess of supply came a drastic drop in prices. Farm income fell from $17.7 billion in 1919 to $10.5 billion in 1921. For the farmers, this was a depression that would last throughout the 1920s and beyond.

Other problems plagued the era as well. With passage in 1919 of the 18th Amendment and the Volstead Act, the manufacturing and sale of alcohol was declared

17

Al Capone

Crowds celebrate the Russian Revolution in Leningrad, April 18, 1917.

illegal in America. Not willing to give up the luxury of drink, many people found ways to get around the law. Bootlegging of alcohol—that is, its illegal manufacture and sale—became a prosperous and widespread enterprise. Since this practice was against the law, it was organized and controlled by gangsters and criminals, the most infamous of whom was Al "Scarface" Capone. Bootlegging was big business, and the greed and criminality of those involved led to numerous incidents of violence.

This period also saw the heyday of the "Red Scare"—a heightened fear of communism, labor-union activity, and racial

and ethnic minorities. This phenomenon had a number of causes, not least of which were the attempts of big-business and government leaders to keep wage and price levels down and to portray the efforts of labor unions as un-American. The success of the Russian Revolution in 1917 and the increasing popularity of socialism in Europe—particularly in Germany—led Americans to fear that recent immigrants, particularly Jews, would seek to spread socialism or communism in the U.S. In addition, there was an increased presence of blacks in industrial jobs and a growing fear among whites that blacks would take jobs away from them by working for lower wages. Thus, in the broad and complex fabric of American life, this time of postwar optimism was also one of labor violence, anti-Semitism, and renewed racial strife.

Though 1923 brought sadness with the death of Harding, business continued to flourish and dreams of wealth were more abundant then ever before. When Vice-President Calvin Coolidge took office to replace Harding, the transition was smooth and uneventful. Like Harding, Coolidge was a great believer in the isolationist approach to foreign policy. He wanted no part in foreign conflicts, only peace and prosperity at home. In some ways, Coolidge, the stone-faced, serious Yankee from Vermont, exemplified all the qualities Americans yearned for in a president. In 1924, riding the wave of prosperity he had inherited, Coolidge ran for the presidency with the slogan "The business of America is business" and was elected.

Calvin Coolidge

The Florida Land Boom

The infamous Florida land boom of 1924-25 is a good illustration of the dangers and effects of massive, irrational speculation. The conditions that governed this phenomenon were similar to those that brought about the stock-market crash five years later.

It seemed that all of a sudden, in the middle of the 1920s, interest in buying Florida real estate reached epidemic proportions. Because of Florida's favorable climate, its accessibility to the big Northeastern cities, and the great increase in the mobility of the American public through the advent of the automobile, Florida became *the* state in which to buy land. Word soon got around that purchasing real estate in Florida was a foolproof investment. A "speculative bubble" was soon created. Everyone was sure that Florida land prices would skyrocket in no time. This confidence caused a rush to buy land, driving prices higher and higher, as demand grew and supply fell. Soon, land in Florida became so valuable that even swampland, bogs, and common scrubland sold for prices greatly in excess of any true value.

This was mostly "speculative" investment; that is, most people were buying the land with no intention of ever living on it. It was bought simply to be sold for a quick turn-around profit: Buy today, sell tomorrow. Land prices rose and rose until the spring of 1926, when the supply of new buyers, essential to maintaining rising prices, began to run dry.

Two serious hurricanes then hit. The worst was on September 18, 1926. It killed 400 people, tore the roofs off countless homes, and piled tons of water and elegant yachts into the streets of Miami. It was not only a natural disaster that struck but a financial one as well. Great amounts of money were lost overnight. Previously valuable investments were now worthless rivers of wreckage.

Somehow this disaster did not dampen the spirit of large-scale speculation. And speculators were soon to turn to another preoccupation, the stock market, in hopes of making millions from a few shrewd and timely investments.

Devastation in the wake of the Miami hurricane.

Library of Congress

At the end of his second term, in 1928, with the country seeming to prosper and the stock market soaring, Coolidge announced that he would not seek another term of office. His presidency had been a relatively happy one, but he was tired.

On December 4, 1928, Coolidge delivered his last State of the Union address. His sentiments were clearly filled with reassurance and optimism: "No Congress of the United States ever assembled, on surveying the state of the union, has met with a more pleasing prospect than that which appears at the present time. In the domestic field there is tranquillity and contentment . . . and the highest record of years of prosperity."

To the average observer, Coolidge's words rang with unquestionable truth. Production and employment were high and rising. Though wages had not gone up along with profits, prices were fairly stable. Many Americans were still very poor, a fact that most of the country refused to acknowledge, but a majority of the citizenry felt better off than ever.

HERBERT HOOVER
FOR PRESIDENT

2

THE BEGINNING OF THE END

After Coolidge's decision not to seek re-election, the Republicans turned to his Secretary of Commerce for leadership. Their man was Herbert Hoover.

Hoover was elected in 1928, and it was during his presidency that America's hopes began to fade. Though many of the foundations for trouble were laid before Hoover took office, he was the unfortunate incumbent during the collapse that was soon to follow.

A few years before Hoover took office, speculation and investment in the stock

Herbert Hoover

market had begun to grow. Along with low interest rates, optimistic statements and assurances from prominent businessmen added to the growing confidence in the market and thus sparked greater activity.

Soon, market activity grew to great proportions. An epidemic of "get rich quick" fever had gripped investors. There came so much investment, and prices rose to such great heights, that many economists and businessmen could already see that a day of reckoning was growing closer. Also, the widespread use of margin—or buying stocks on credit—created a condition in which many investors had overextended themselves.

Think of the problem this way: You have just received a brand-new credit card. You hear that the department stores in your area are having incredible sales on their merchandise. With very little money in the bank, you go out and charge $1,000 worth of merchandise on your new card. Everything is wonderful—until the bill comes. Suppose many others did exactly what you had done. Soon, the credit-card company would go bankrupt and not be able to pay the department stores. The department stores would then go out of business, in turn putting all of the businesses that supplied them with goods out of business as well. The whole system would collapse. This is essentially what happened with margin buying in the Stock Market. Many investors used their "credit cards" (margin) without money to back it up.

To add to this dilemma, speculation became so out of control that stocks were being sold with incredible rapidity. Shares were traded so fast, and the money made from their sale was reinvested so quickly, that most "profits" were only figures on a piece of paper.

There was, in theory, one control to slow down this dangerous spiral of speculation. The control lay in the hands of the Federal Reserve Board—commonly known as the "Fed." Since the Fed controls the amount of money in the economy, its control on the stock market is relatively simple:

1. The Fed offers banks money at rates of interest just as private banks offer money to the public at rates of interest.

2. Private banks lend money to brokers so that brokers can cover the values of stocks bought on margin.

3. In return, the banks receive interest rates from brokers higher than those they must pay to the government.

Since the private banks borrow money from the Fed, the rate of interest from private banks depends on the rate of interest the bank must pay. If the Fed raises

Charlotte McGuinn Freeman

View of the Federal Reserve Bank, New York.

its rates to private banks, the private banks must raise their rates for their customers.

4. If Fed rates are high, so are rates all the way down the line. High rates decrease investment and speculation in the market because brokers cannot afford to borrow as much as when rates are lower.

In February 1927 the Federal Reserve Board did raise its rates, in an effort to curb the massive activity in the stock market. Unfortunately, this action had little effect. The Fed raised interest rates again in May, and still there was no visible effect. The system had somehow gone out of control. Later, as the dangers grew more and more threatening, the Fed declared that money given to bankers should not be used for speculative purposes. This caused a brief decrease in speculation, with a brief decrease in prices, but soon the activity would rise again, stronger and more dangerous than ever before.

By 1929, some effects of this boundless growth were becoming apparent. Speculative activity was so great that bank loans to brokers rose from $1.5 billion in 1923 to $6 billion in 1929, and the number of stockbrokers nationwide jumped from 30,000 in 1920 to 71,000 by the end of 1929.

While the market chugged blindly along, certain danger signs showed themselves in the summer of 1929. The construction industry, usually an indicator of general business conditions, showed a decline of $1 billion between 1928 and 1929. Industrial production, which peaked in July of 1929, started to decline in August, along with employment.

Now, at the peak of this prosperity, most Americans did not consider that the "dream" would sometime have to end. Though most people were unaware of it, there were many others in the country who were poor. The distribution of wealth at this time was so uneven that 27,500 of the wealthiest families in America had a combined wealth equal to America's 12 million poorest families. Seventy-eight percent of America's families still earned less than $3,000 a year, and yet it was a commonly accepted belief that the people who did not take advantage of America's great wave of prosperity were lazy or stupid, or both.

The stock market suffered a few mild declines in September of 1929, but the unfailing confidence of investors continued, miraculously, to smooth out these setbacks. Unaware of the disaster that was about to befall them, investors, speculators, brokers, and other participants stood eagerly by, waiting for prices to rise to even higher levels.

3

RICHES TO RAGS

In October of 1929, the economic monster America had created began to rear its ugly head. During the early part of the month, there were some unexpected declines in stock prices. It was expected that a recovery would swiftly take place, as it had in the recent past. But this time the recovery did not come.

On Thursday, October 24—soon to be known as "Black Thursday," stocks opened at moderately steady prices. Then the selling began. The rate of sales became rapid, and prices began to fall. Before the first hour of trading was over, it was clear that prices were dropping faster than they ever had before.

Where was this sudden flood of selling coming from? Most likely, forced selling by brokers who had overextended and exhausted margin to their clients was the primary cause. They now needed cash to cover their financial responsibilities.

Fear and panic were soon to follow. As prices fell, investors and speculators wanted to sell as fast as they could, hoping to get out of the market before their stocks became worthless. Confusion engulfed the floor of the Exchange.

At noon, a meeting of some of the country's most prominent and powerful bankers was called, to be held in the offices of J. P. Morgan & Co. Aware of the emergency at

John Pierpont Morgan

hand, the bankers decided that it was time to organize support to save the market from an even more severe fate. It was resolved that each of the banks represented would contribute $40 million to a money pool that would then be used to buy stocks at reasonable prices. This, they thought, would end the panic and stop the dangerous wave of selling. For a while, they were right.

When news of the meeting leaked out, prices began to level off. Prices held for Friday and Saturday, and since the Exchange was closed on Sunday, many thought the day off would give the market a chance to regain its balance.

On Monday, when the market reopened, prices fell even more drastically than they had on Black Thursday. Again, the bankers assembled at the Morgan office. But this time there was no help to be given. The bankers would not again come to the rescue of the market.

Tuesday, October 29, was the bleakest day in the 112-year history of the New York Stock Exchange. More than 16 million shares of stock changed hands, and many stocks closed at half the value they showed that morning.

News spread quickly that bankers were selling stocks to try to avoid being wiped out financially. Prices were to fall even lower, but the great volume of trading and loss would never again be as great. It was mid-November before the market reached its absolute bottom. By this time, most stocks on the Exchange had suffered enormous losses in value.

At first it was thought that the Crash of '29 and the Depression that followed would be short-lived, however severe. After all, the U.S. had endured occasional depressions and stock-market scares in the past. But this decline and fall came harder and faster, and lasted longer, than any America had ever seen.

Stockbrokers were now heavily in debt to banks for money they had borrowed to

Crowds rush to withdraw money from failing banks.

cover margin purchases. Brokers sent out "margin calls" to thousands of their clients, requesting cash for the margin they had used. The brokers had no choice. Stock prices were so low that even if the broker sold the stocks he had purchased for his clients, he would not be able to raise enough money to cover his debts to the banks.

Most clients who received the pleas for money had no money to give. Corporations and banks that had invested heavily in the market suffered greatly as well. When the banks asked the brokers for repayment of outstanding loans, most brokers had no choice but to default. This caused a great shortage of money in the banks, and often banks could not raise enough cash for the depositors to withdraw.

Though enormous sums of money were lost as a result of the stock-market collapse, the crash was not the sole factor in the creation of the economic depression that now plagued the country.

During the time of great prosperity, businesses kept prices and profits high and kept increasing the volume of goods they produced. At the same time, wages were kept low, which meant that the great majority of people were held back in their ability to purchase these goods. So, by 1929, there were great quantities of goods to be had, at artificially high prices, with fewer and fewer people able to buy them. This led to a surplus of goods as well as of the means to produce them, which caused business and industry to close down facilities and, of course, to lay off large numbers of workers.

The dilemma for farming was much the same as that for industry. Having greatly raised production levels during World War I, farmers maintained high production even after the war, when demand dropped drastically. This caused surpluses; that is, more food was being produced than could be sold at market prices. Now farmers had to accept greatly reduced prices for their goods and, in turn, had little money to consume goods produced in other industries.

By the spring of 1930, six months after the crash, more than 4 million Americans were out of work. The alarming effects of unemployment became evident with lines around the block at most employment agencies across the country. Men and women who used to be "good providers" now stood on "bread lines," waiting anxiously for a bowl of watery soup and a crust of stale bread. Children were starving. Bands of homeless men slept outside, huddled together around campfires built of scraps and debris. In New York, men built cardboard huts along the Hudson River. Gangs of desperate souls were seen fighting over choice morsels salvaged from garbage cans or municipal dumps.

By the beginning of the winter of 1931, unemployment had reached 8 million. By December, it had climbed to 13.5 million, almost one third of the American labor force. Jobless, penniless, and without hope, many "hit the road," riding boxcars, traveling to nowhere in particular.

Between 1930 and 1931, the problem worsened for farmers as well. Farm prices had fallen more than 30 percent. Corn sold for 15¢ a bushel, cotton and wool for 5¢ a pound, pork was 3¢ a pound, and beef was sold at 2½¢ a pound. Though the prices farmers could get for their goods fell, their expenses did not. The farmer's taxes and mortgages had been figured in the 1920s, when farming brought much higher income. A farmer who had borrowed, for example, $1,000 on a mortgage when wheat sold for 15¢ a bushel, owed, in effect, 6,666 bushels of wheat. But, as the bottom fell out of the market and prices dropped to 5¢ a bushel, the farmer found

himself owing 20,000 bushels of wheat on his mortgage.

Banks, which had a shortage of funds, could not wait for farmers to regain prosperity and were forced to confiscate land and other belongings, putting them up for auction to sell at whatever price they would bring. The American farmer would then join the ranks of the homeless who wandered the country, dazed and confused, and uncertain of what lay ahead.

As the second winter of the Depression descended, local relief organizations such as the Red Cross and the Salvation Army began to run out of money under the incredible strain of nationwide need. It seemed that now only the federal government could help. But pleas to the government fell mostly upon deaf ears. Herbert Hoover continued to uphold his belief that the government should have no place in aiding the unfortunate. The president felt that federal aid to the needy would undermine the initiative of the unemployed to find work. He feared that the government would become one gigantic charity and the country's hardship cases would grow completely dependent on government "handouts." All Hoover could do was continue to issue optimistic statements to the public

An Oklahoma farmer and his sons take shelter from a dust storm.

Red Cross volunteer dispenses food to drought victims in Lonoke, Arkansas, 1931.

about the new prosperity soon to come. He asserted that the Depression would soon "blow over."

The lack of action on the part of Hoover and his administration soon caused the nation to grow dangerously angry and frustrated. On March 19, 1930, 1,110 men standing on a bread line in New York City seized two truckloads of bread and rolls that were to be delivered to a nearby hotel. In Henryetta, Oklahoma, in July of 1931, 300 jobless men threatened to beat and kill local storekeepers unless the merchants supplied them with food. Looting and violence became widespread. The realities of starvation, unemployment, and a feeling of worthlessness transformed once-law-abiding citizens into violent beings.

Hoover's attitude continued to be one of neglect. The president continued to issue unrealistic statements about the state of the country. "Nobody," he told newspapers, "is actually starving. The hobos, for example, are better fed now than they have ever been."

By 1932, unemployment exceeded 14

million and was still rising. Bread lines now
included citizens who were once con-
sidered well off. Businessmen, storekeepers, and middle-class housewives had
joined the ranks of the stricken. Need was
so great that relief agencies could not begin to ease the problem. In Chicago, half
the city's labor force was unemployed. In
the Pennsylvania coal fields, miners were
forced to live on roots and dandelions.
Weeds were common fare in Kentucky.
More and more children were dying of
starvation.

Another attempt on behalf of laborers to
find work came on March 7, 1932, in Dearborn, Michigan. In the midst of freezing
temperatures, 3,000 jobless men marched
on the shut-down Ford plant at River

*Violence erupts during the Dearborn strike,
Dearborn, Michigan, 1932.*

The Bonus Army

In 1932, a group of World War I veterans assembled in Portland, Oregon, to form an organization called the Bonus Expeditionary Force (BEF), also known as the Bonus Army. Those who gathered decided that since they were living on the edge of starvation, they would demand immediate payment of bonuses promised to them by Congress for their service in the war. Congress had voted, just after the war, to pay these men bonuses in 1945, but for these starving and demoralized men, 1945 was too far away.

The members of the BEF chose a former sergeant named Walter W. Waters as their spokesman. It was decided that their cause would be publicized by marching on Washington and petitioning Congress and the president for prompt payment of what was owed them. Realizing the controversy they might stir, the marchers were careful to maintain strict discipline throughout their efforts. They advocated "no panhandling, no drinking, and no radicalism."

Many journeyed to Washington, D.C., by hitchhiking; some hopped freight trains. By the time Waters and his men reached the Capitol, their number had grown to about a thousand. As the days and weeks of camping out near the Capitol at Anacostia Flats went by, the BEF's forces grew to more than 15,000 veterans and their families.

The House of Representatives began debating a bill that would provide for swift payment of bonuses. On June 15, 1932, with the BEF still camped out nearby, the House passed the bill. But the victory was not yet won. The Senate was not so easy to convince.

The Senate felt the Bonus Army was a threat and believed that giving in to their demands would be "knuckling under" to pressure from a mob. On June 17, the Bonus Bill came up for a vote on the floor of the Senate. Thousands of veterans gathered outside the Capitol building, waiting to hear the outcome. President Hoover, feeling uneasy about the mob outside, was preparing to call out the U.S. Army.

After hours of anticipation, the word was out. Mr. Waters stood up in the crowd to give his men the verdict. "Comrades," he announced, "I have bad news." The bill had been defeated.

A moment passed. No one was sure what the next move would be. Then, in an ironic display of patriotism born of frustration and exhaustion, the crowd began to sing "America." Then the crowd quietly dispersed and returned to their shanties in Anacostia Flats. There, most stayed on, having nowhere in particular to go. Some hit the road once more. Congress would soon adjourn, and the issue would be dead forever.

Hoover continued to deny access to any member or representative of the BEF who wished to be heard in the White House. The president also felt that the still large group encamped so near the Capitol was not only a threat to American government but also an unsightly collection of misfortunates who only underscored the nation's growing epidemic of poverty. The veterans were ordered to clear out.

Word was sent from the White House to Douglas MacArthur, then Army chief of staff, to use troops in an effort to empty Anacostia Flats of its inhabitants. MacArthur picked up his riding crop, summoned his aide, Major Dwight D. Eisenhower, mounted his horse, and started off for the Bonus Army encampment.

MacArthur's force arrived with tanks, swords, bayonets, and tear gas. They granted the veterans exactly one hour to grab their tattered belongings and evacuate the area. As night fell, the troops moved in. Soldiers began harassing and mauling the veterans who held their ground. The cardboard and tarpaper shanties that once housed the BEF members were destroyed and burned. The unarmed BEF did not give the troops much of a fight. Most were too stunned to see that men who wore the same uniforms once worn by the veterans themselves had now turned against them.

By midnight, Bonus City, which had once housed more than 15,000 of the country's homeless and jobless, was a field of roaring flames. In an attempt to explain the violence, Hoover declared that the BEF was a mob of criminals and communists, saying, "A challenge to the authority of the United State government has been met swiftly and firmly. Our government cannot be coerced by mob rule."

Left, *the Bonus Army marches to the Capitol.* Below left, *the Bonus Army camped on the Capitol lawn.* Below right, *General MacArthur leading the U.S. Army into Anacostia Flats.*

Two young inhabitants of "Hooverville"

Rouge. Demanding work, they wished to present a petition at the plant. When they reached the factory, Dearborn police were waiting. The marchers were ordered to turn back. When the marchers pressed the police, they were met with tear gas. The workers fought back with rocks and pieces of ice. Finally, the Ford Company fire department released tons of icy-cold, high-pressure water on the protesters. In addition, the police opened gunfire. The crowd fled in panic, leaving behind four dead and many wounded.

In 1932, Hoover decided to take limited action. He conceived and implemented the Reconstruction Finance Corporation (RFC), which was authorized to lend money to banks and to businesses in order to keep them in operation. At first, the loans were made secretly. The reason for this was the government's fear that confidence in banks would be lost when the public learned of their getting "handouts" from the government. Rumors about crooked operations spread, and soon Congress forced the RFC to disclose its records.

Although the RFC was able to keep a number of businesses afloat and to hold off further collapse of the economy, the Hoover administration had still done nothing directly to help the millions of people in need. By 1932, public resentment toward the once-popular Hoover reached great proportions. The clusters of tarpaper houses, or "shantytowns," were now called "Hoovervilles." Broken-down automobiles hauled by mules were called "Hoover wagons," empty pockets called "Hoover-flags," and discarded newspapers renamed "Hoover blankets." The man in the White House became a symbol of everything the public now dreaded about life in America.

4

AMERICANS GET A "NEW DEAL"

With the Depression and the daily crises that accompanied it, many people began to realize that drastic change was unavoidable. New philosophies about social justice and reform took hold. Programs to provide better working conditions and more money for labor were being proposed. Social reformers believed they were now in a race against time. If something was not changed soon, America could collapse further into chaos or even, perhaps, into revolution.

Since 1932 was an election year, the logical place to turn was to the Democrats.

Secretary of the Navy, Franklin Delano Roosevelt

Leading the party against Hoover's Republican administration was the governor of New York, Franklin Delano Roosevelt.

From the outset of the 1932 campaign, it was clear that there were many differences between Roosevelt and Hoover, in both political thought and personal style. Roosevelt had been born into an old, aristocratic family of New York's Hudson River Valley. Whereas Hoover was a practical, self-made farmer's son from Iowa, Roosevelt had been reared in the ways of *politesse* (quiet decorum) and *noblesse oblige* (the idea that the privileged should act generously and responsibly toward the public). As a popular governor of New

York State from 1928-1932, Roosevelt implemented at the state level the belief of fellow "reform Democrats" that government should come to the aid of victims of economic hardship. As early as 1929, the governor's relief programs included aid to farmers, regulation of utilities prices, and pension plans for the elderly. With the deepening of the depression, by 1931 Roosevelt began to hire as advisers a number of scholars and experts in government and economics. The purpose of this was to begin to design an overall program of social welfare and reform, for it was the governor's strong belief that entirely new programs would be needed to save the American system of private enterprise from collapse. Thus was born the famous "Brain Trust" of the Roosevelt presidency.

Roosevelt was elected president in November, 1932, winning the electoral votes of all but six states. By Inauguration Day, March 4, 1933, more than 15 million employable Americans were out of work. After being sworn in at the inaugural ceremony, Franklin Delano Roosevelt spoke to the nation for the first time as president. Millions of Americans stood eagerly by, awaiting words of encouragement and de-

Roosevelt, Dr. Alexander and Rexford Tugwell tour Greenbelt, the experimental model community they planned outside of Washington, D.C., 1937.

Franklin D. Roosevelt's first inauguration, March 4, 1933.

termination, and the new president delivered one of the most memorable speeches in American history, saying, in part:

> "Let me assert my firm belief that the only thing we have to fear is fear itself—nameless, unreasoning, unjustified terror which paralyzes needed efforts to convert retreat into advance. This nation asks for action, and asks for action now."

With these words, a new approach to the problems of economic depression was born.

The task that Roosevelt undertook was enormous. The problem that required his earliest attention was the collapse of the banking system. The majority of the banks in the country had closed, along with the Chicago Grain Exchange and the New York Stock Exchange. Only four hours after his inauguration, Roosevelt called his Secretary of the Treasury, William Woodin, and ordered him to draft emergency legislation relating to the regulation of banks. The following day, two executive orders were issued: The first proclaimed a national "bank holiday," which provided for the closing of the banks that were still open, in order to prevent depositors from withdrawing all their money; the second order prohibited the export of gold. These two swift actions stopped virtually all economic activity and gave the new administration some time to plan action. An emergency session of Congress was called for March 9.

Experts and legislators worked day and night in their efforts to devise a program that would revive the banking system.

Cartoon run in the Camden Post, Camden, N.J., March 14, 1933.

F.D.R. broadcasting one of his famous "Fireside Chats"

Finally, a bill was ready. The bill extended government assistance to private banks and gave the president complete control over gold shipments. It also granted the power to issue new currency through the Federal Reserve Banks and placed the failed banks into the hands of the federal government. Thus the government would conduct the orderly reopening of banks that still had sufficient funds left in their vaults.

On Sunday evening, March 12, Americans turned on their radios to hear Roosevelt's first "fireside chat," an informal, friendly address to the nation. Over the airwaves came the encouraging words that America's banks were once again secure and safe for deposits. So powerful and influential was Roosevelt's message that the next day, when the banks reopened their doors, deposits actually exceeded withdrawals. Confidence had been restored.

Even more popular than the first fireside chat was the message sent on March 13, which called for an amendment to the Volstead Act, the bill that made the manufacture and sale of alcohol illegal. The amended act would legalize the sale of beer, and soon after, all alcohol was once again made legal with passage of the Twenty-first Amendment to the Constitution.

For the next few months, Roosevelt's administration undertook a massive program of legislation that was to affect practically all areas of American life. Known since then as the "Hundred Days," this period changed forever the role of government in American society.

The most significant programs created and implemented by FDR's administration were carried out by the following acts and organizations, each abbreviated with three or four initials and known collectively as FDR's "alphabet agencies."

Agricultural Adjustment Act (AAA)

To bring aid to ailing farmers, the AAA provided a means by which farm prices could be supported by the government. In practice, the government actually paid the farmers to *cut down* on production. This was done to cause a rise in prices for the goods. The AAA also empowered the president to sell any surplus farm products on the world market for whatever price they would bring.

Farm Credit Administration (FCA)

Further enhancing the goals of the AAA, the FCA essentially made the federal government a bank for American farmers. The FCA refinanced farm mortgages throughout the nation, buying old mortgages away from the banks and insurance companies and lowering the interest payments to halt the epidemic of farm foreclosures.

Cotton farm, Mississippi Delta, 1937

Library of Congress

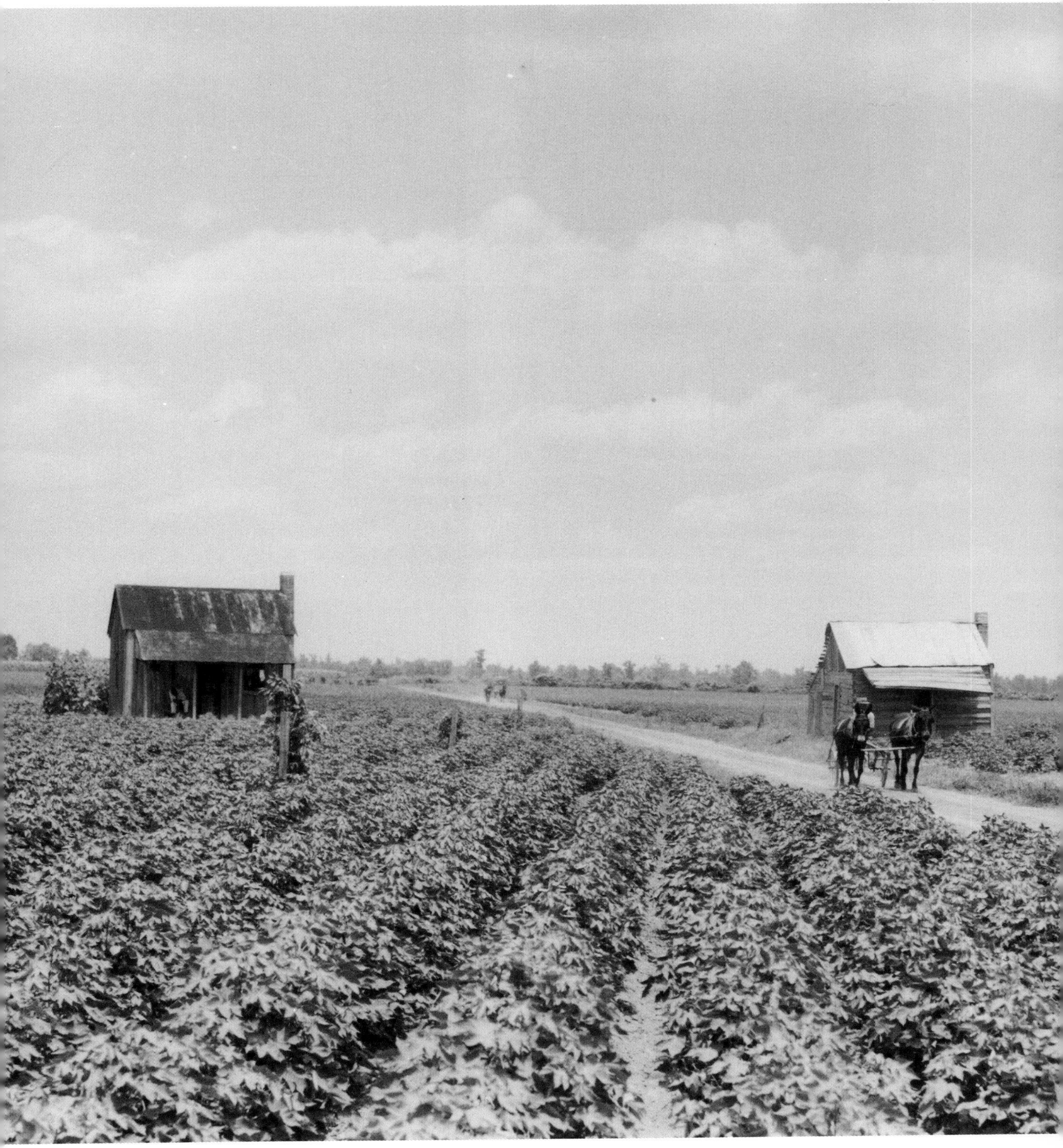

President Roosevelt and advisers lunching at a CCC Camp at Big Meadows, Virginia, August, 1933.

Civilian Conservation Corps (CCC)

The CCC provided an opportunity for Roosevelt to combine his passion for conservation of natural resources with his desire to improve the lives of the unemployed, particularly the young and out of work.

The CCC would provide hundreds of thousands of the unemployed with jobs of physical labor in an effort to preserve the nation's physical heritage. When FDR was informed that the CCC would not provide significant relief in the long run, the president added a proposal to grant $500 million to state relief organizations in addition to the creation of the CCC. Eight days later, the CCC was law, and soon 300,000 young men were hard at work under the supervision of the U.S. Army and the Labor Department.

All across the nation, the CCC worked on land clearance, forestry, dam construction, and the improvement of national parks. Eventually, two and a half million workers passed through the ranks of the CCC.

The CCC was a popular creation, but the $500 million proposed for the relief organizations sparked controversy from the members of Congress who still felt, as Hoover had, that relief was still a local responsibility, not a federal one. Nonetheless, after much debate, the Federal Emergency Relief Administration (FERA) was created to distribute the $500 million to those in need.

CCC workers planting trees

Tennessee Valley Authority (TVA)

Proposed by FDR in April 1933, the TVA was to provide cheap electrical power to farmers, manufacture cheap fertilizer, and work on preventing floods and soil erosion in the Tennessee Valley. All this would be accomplished by giving the government control of the Muscle Shoals electric and nitrogen power plant, which had been built at public expense on the Tennessee River during World War I. The TVA was enacted on May 18.

Home Owner's Loan Corporation (HOLC)

Brought to Congress for consideration on June 13, the HOLC was proposed as an institution that would refinance home mortgages for those who had lost their homes as far back as 1930. Within months of the bill's passage by Congress, one out of every ten Americans had mortgaged his home through the HOLC. The new rise in home ownership and financing brought an improvement in both the real-estate and construction industries.

National Recovery Administration (NRA)

Perhaps the most significant measure proposed by Roosevelt, and the one closest to his heart, was the NRA. Controversial and innovative, the NRA brought American business and American government into a partnership unlike any that had existed before. Adopted in Congress on June 15, the National Recovery Administration—originally the National Industrial Recovery Act (NIRA)—was an experiment in cooperation between the government and business in hopes of providing wider employment as well as more affordable goods for the country. The "three R's" were the key: relief, reform, and recovery.

First, big business requested an easing of anti-trust laws, originally enacted in 1890 as the Sherman Anti-Trust Act. These laws prohibited businesses in a given industry from conspiring with one another to control the prices of their goods. By agreeing together to set a level of pro-

Cartoon depicting the cooperation between Government, Management and Worker under the NRA.

Library of Congress

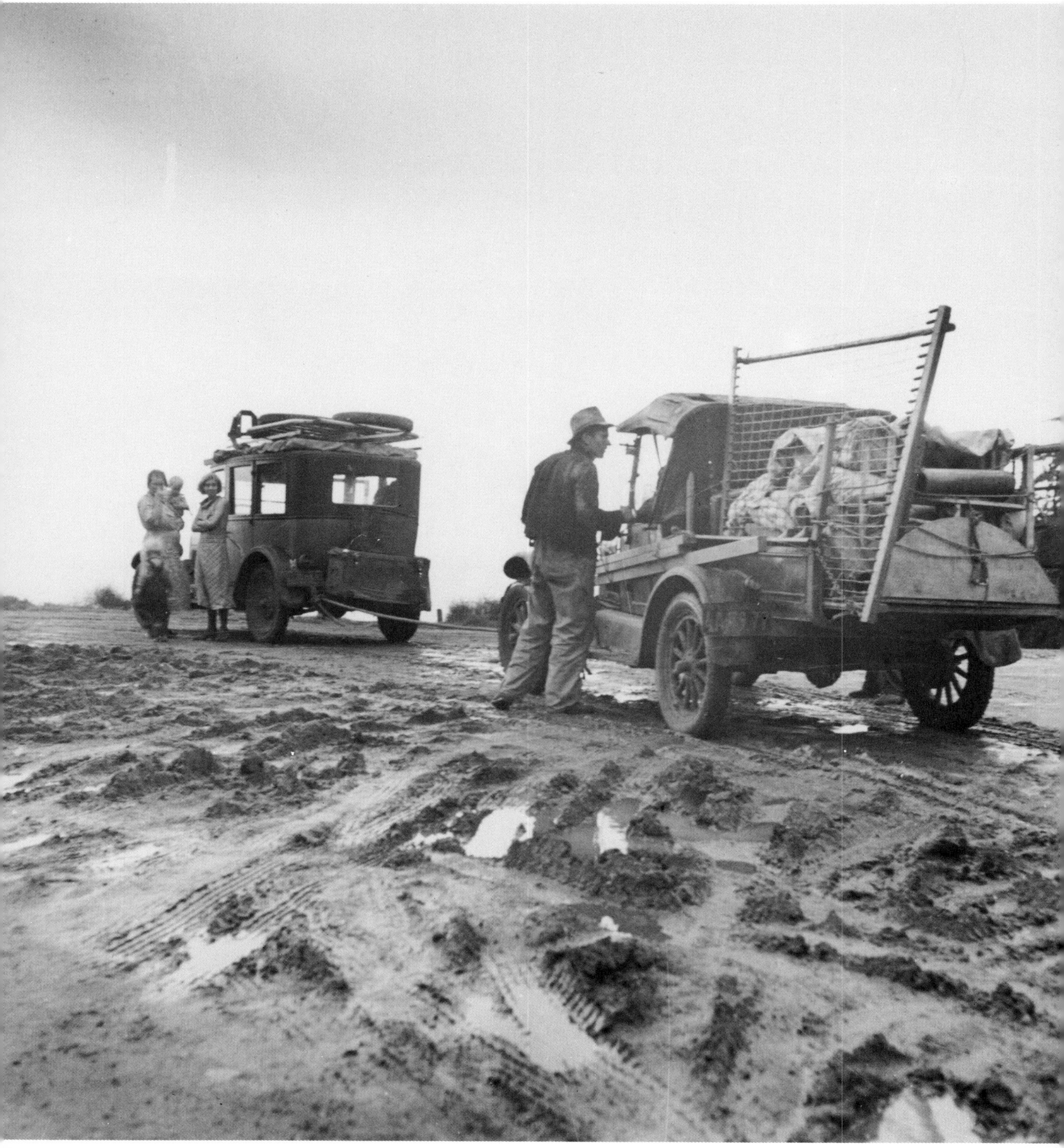

duction output, these businesses were able to control not only the supply of a given product but also the price. This practice was contrary to the idea of fair competition, in which demand in the marketplace would naturally regulate the price and supply of goods.

With the creation of the NRA, big business argued that in order to achieve recovery, large corporations must be allowed to work together to plan for the future and set worldwide standards for production and price. The Roosevelt administration agreed, but only on the condition that the government would have the authority to regulate the standards.

Businessmen were then required to obtain government authorization to enforce "codes" regulating production, pricing, and fair-competition practices for each industry. The government would license only those businesses that agreed to a minimum wage and a maximum number of hours in a work week. In addition, businesses would have to grant employees the right to organize and bargain collectively—that is, to unionize.

By the time Congress adjourned on June 16, one hundred days after the emergency session was called by FDR, fifteen major laws and countless minor ones had been adopted. This new legislation basically created a level of interaction between government and private business that had never before existed in the United States.

By 1934, the economy had begun to show some signs of improvement. Unemployment was still widespread, but national income in 1934 was 50 percent higher than it was in 1933, and some 5 million previously unemployed Americans had found work. Full economic recovery was still years away, but the sense of crisis and hopelessness that had gripped the nation for so long had begun to ease.

Homeless families search for work in the California pea fields.

AFTERWORD

ANOTHER CHALLENGE

While America focused on rebuilding during the 1930s, developments in Europe continued to be troubling. Crippled by the destruction of World War I, Europe in the 1920s was left with many towns and cities destroyed and its economy in ruins. In Germany, massive inflation and a lack of jobs caused people to suffer from many of the same frustrations and fears that plagued Americans during the 1930s.

Just as Americans were desperate for an answer to their problems in their time of fear, so too were the German people.

Adolf Hitler

Roosevelt was the answer for many Americans; for the Germans, the answer was Adolf Hitler and his National Socialists—the Nazi party.

Both Hitler and Roosevelt promised economic prosperity and a bright future for their respective nations. Roosevelt sought solutions through innovative programs and a new involvement of government in industry. Adolf Hitler and the Nazis calmed the panic of their country with assurances of German-Aryan superiority. Jews in particular were singled out not only as inferior humans but also as the cause of Germany's problems.

Hitler was worshipped as a savior. In

Following page, Nazi rally spells out name of border province lost in World War I later returned to Germany in March, 1935.

turn, he offered his followers the pride and thrill of conquest that had been denied them in World War I.

In the years 1932 to 1936, Hitler and the Nazi party gained complete control of the German government. The task they undertook was one of strengthening Germany's army and creating a massive military state. The nation was preparing for war, and with this preparation came new economic growth from the now-booming military industry.

In the United States, Hitler's program went largely ignored. Though the world grew increasingly wary of the Nazis' intentions, in the U.S., Britain, and elsewhere, fear of reliving the horrors of World War I kept these nations from getting involved.

By the end of his first presidential term, Roosevelt was fighting political battles at home. A rise in opposition from big business and the rich began to threaten his chances for reelection in 1936. The wealthy realized that Roosevelt was determined to bring a real change in the structure of the American economy, a change that would limit the levels of profit they could make. When taxes were raised on the rich in 1935, hatred toward FDR grew even stronger. Roosevelt was called "a traitor to his class," a "dictator," and a "communist."

The Republicans chose Alfred Mossman Landon, governor of Kansas, to lead their fight for the White House. A wealthy independent oil producer who, it was thought, would appeal to the rich and big business, Landon's platform was one of the "regular guy" who had no thoughts of being a "dictator." After a long campaign and many bad words between the parties, Roosevelt was reelected by a landslide. FDR's victory came partly as a result of the fact that many of those who were impoverished by The Great Depression felt that FDR and the Democrats were helping to ease their hardships.

Still, 1936 was riddled with troubles elsewhere in the world. Hitler's army had marched into the demilitarized zone between France and Germany—the Rhineland—and had remilitarized it. Italy, under fascist dictator Benito Mussolini, had invaded Ethiopia, in northeastern Africa, and occupied its capital. Francisco

Alfred M. ("Alf") Landon, presidential candidate, 1936

56

Benito Mussolini

*Women welders build fuselage
for Boeing B-17.*

Franco, a Spanish general backed by the Germans and Italians, was drawing close to Madrid in an effort to take over the democratic government of Spain.

The threat of the German-Italian alliance was now becoming increasingly clear to the world. Public opinion in the U.S. began to awaken as news of the fascist takeovers spread. Though the idea of entering another war still met with disfavor, it was becoming obvious that nonparticipation would soon become difficult, if not impossible.

In his annual message to Congress in 1939, Roosevelt appealed to all Americans for unity in the face of foreign threats. In addition, he called for a rapid build-up in U.S. military arms.

Soon after FDR's speech, Czechoslovakia was seized by the Germans and Albania invaded by Mussolini. With Germany's invasion of Poland and, in 1940, its bombing of southern England and the ensuing Battle of Britain, it was clear that the U.S. could not stay out of the fray for long.

It was in December 1941, with the Japanese attack on Pearl Harbor, that the U.S. became officially engaged in World War II. But by that time, the U.S. had begun its preparation for war by increasing production of military goods at home and by providing supplies to its allies—particularly Great Britain—in the war in Europe. By the end of the 1930s, the decade-long crisis of the Depression was being replaced by the crisis of world war. Though it is true that the growth in industrial production as a preparation for war aided the U.S. in its recovery, it is equally the case that without the economic innovations of the early years of the New Deal, 1933-1936, the economic and political systems of the U.S. might not have been preserved.

Thus, the tale of the Crash and the Depression, from that Black Thursday in 1929 to the devastating spread of poverty, to a new threat of war by 1939, is one of perseverence and change, and of the durability of America's government and its people.

INDEX

Page numbers in *italics* indicate illustrations

SUGGESTED READING

HACKER, JEFFREY H. *Franklin D. Roosevelt.* New York: Lothrop, Lee and Shepard Books, 1981.

MELTZER, MILTON. *Brother, Can You Spare A Dime? The Great Depression 1929-1933.* New York: Alfred A. Knopf, 1969.

RAWCLIFFE, MICHAEL. *The Roosevelt File.* North Pomfret, VT: David and Charles Inc., 1980.

SULLIVAN, WILSON. *Franklin Delano Roosevelt.* New York: Harper and Row, 1970.

THRASHER, CRYSTAL. *A Taste of Daylight.* New York: Atheneum, 1984.

1 2 3 4 5 6 7 8 9 10—IL—93 92 91 90 89 88 87 86